ABOUT OUR FLAG

BY **Elinor Rees**

ILLUSTRATED BY **Jerome W. Bowen**

Melmont Publishers, Inc., Chicago, Illinois

To Whitman McGowan, who loves to salute the flag his father serves.

Also by Elinor Rees   AT THE BANK

Library of Congress Catalog Card Number 60-5159

TABLE OF CONTENTS Pages

OUR FIRST FLAG

A long, long time ago, when our country was still very new, it had no flag.

General George Washington wanted a flag for his army and for his ships. He could not use one of the colonial flags. That would make one colony seem more important than another. Neither did he wish to use the Grand Union Flag which had flown over his camp at Cambridge. In one corner of that flag was the Union Jack, the King of England's flag.

By the spring of 1776, George Washington and many other Americans wanted independence from Great Britain. They wanted a flag that would be suitable for a new and independent country.

Betsy Ross had an upholstery shop in Philadelphia. One day she was surprised by a visit from George Washington. With him were two other important Americans — George Ross and Robert Morris.

George Ross was a well-known lawyer. He was the uncle of Betsy Ross's dead husband, John. John Ross had died fighting for America.

Robert Morris was a rich man who risked his fortune to help the American cause.

George Washington explained to Betsy Ross that he and his friends were acting as a committee. They were to choose a design for a flag for the new country.

"Mrs. Ross," said George Washington, "do you think you could make a flag like this for us?"

He took from his pocket the drawing of a flag. It had thirteen stripes — seven red and six white. In one corner was a blue field with thirteen stars in a circle. Each stripe and each star stood for one of the thirteen colonies.

Betsy Ross looked at the drawing, then said she would try.

"But why did you draw stars with six points?" she asked. "Five-pointed stars would look better."

George Washington explained that he would need many flags. He thought six-pointed stars would be easier to make.

With that, Betsy Ross picked up a pair of scissors. In a jiffy she had cut a star with five points. So George Washington agreed that the stars should have five instead of six points.

"Mrs. Ross," said the General, "how soon can you finish this flag?"

"Very quickly," she answered.

Betsy Ross knew she would have to work fast. The break with Great Britain might come in a few weeks. It might even come in a few days. The new flag should be ready whenever the break came.

Betsy Ross had never made a flag. She borrowed a flag from Mr. Morris, who was in the shipping business. She studied how the flag was made. Then she went to work.

It took Betsy Ross just one day to make the first American flag.

That was still in the spring of 1776. In that same year, on July 4, 1776, the colonies declared their independence from Great Britain.

After the Declaration of Independence, the thirteen colonies were called states. From that time on, our country was called the United States of America.

On June 14, 1777, the flag that Betsy Ross had made became the official flag of our country. Ever since then, June 14 has been called Flag Day.

Our first flag, the flag that Betsy Ross made for General Washington, flew over his army and from his ships a long, long time ago. The United States of America was a little country then, but it had big hopes and big dreams.

GRAND UNION
FLAG

BETSY ROSS
FLAG

STAR SPANGLED
BANNER

OTHER FLAGS OF THE UNITED STATES

Time went on. Two more states joined the Union. Now the flag had fifteen stars and fifteen stripes. The country grew fast. More states were added. The law makers decided the design of the flag would have to be changed.

In 1818 the people, by voting, said, "From now on the flag shall have just thirteen stripes. They shall stand for the thirteen states with which our country began.

"The stars shall be in rows, not in a circle. There shall be a star for each state in the Union. When a state joins the Union, another star shall be put into the blue field. This shall be done on the Fourth of July after the state has become a part of the United States of America."

10

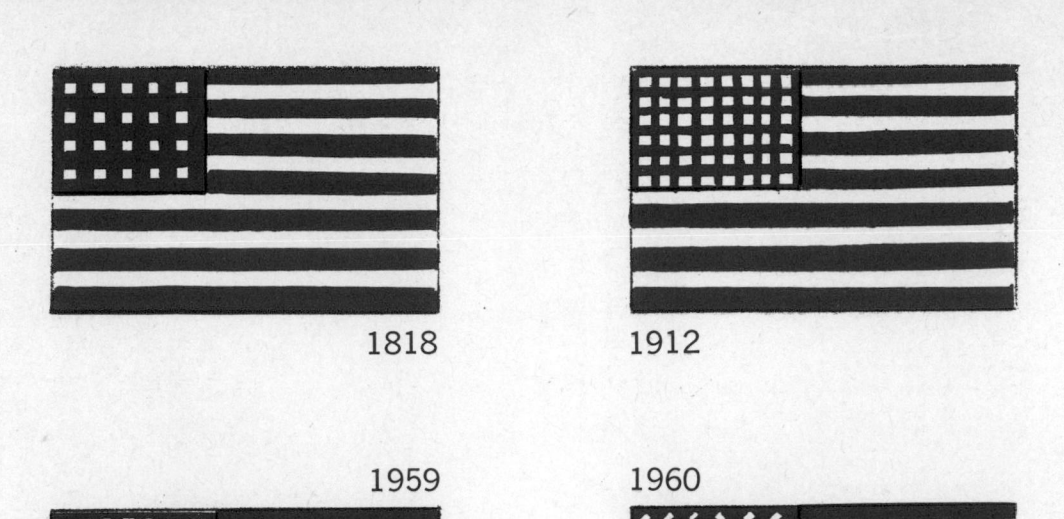

1818   1912

1959   1960

By 1818 there were twenty states. The flag had thirteen stripes and twenty stars. By 1912 the number of stars had increased to forty-eight.

For forty-six years after that the flag remained the same. No state was added to the Union. Then, on January 3, 1959, Alaska became the forty-ninth state. On July 4, 1959, the forty-ninth star was added to the flag.

Hawaii was made a state on August 21, 1959. Now the flag has fifty stars.

Delaware.................1787

New Jersey.................1787

Pennsylvania.................1787

Connecticut.................1788

Georgia.................1788

Maryland.................1788

Massachusetts.................1788

New Hampshire.................1788

New York.................1788

South Carolina.................1788

Virginia.................1788

North Carolina.................1789

Rhode Island.................1790

Vermont.................1791

Kentucky.................1792

Tennessee.................1796

Ohio.................1803

Louisiana.................1812

Indiana.................1816

Mississippi.................1817

Illinois.................1818

Alabama.................1819

Maine.................1820

Missouri.................1821

Arkansas.................1836

Alaska

Hawaii

WERE ADMITTED TO THE UNION

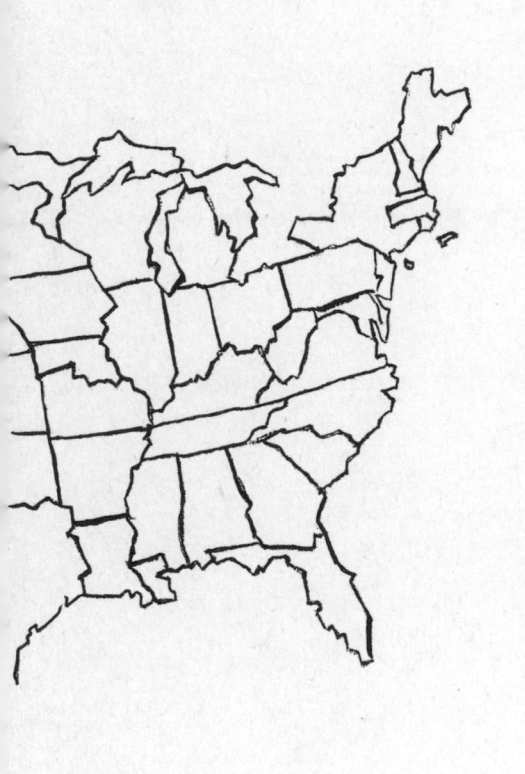

Michigan	1837
Florida	1845
Texas	1845
Iowa	1846
Wisconsin	1848
California	1850
Minnesota	1858
Oregon	1859
Kansas	1861
West Virginia	1863
Nevada	1864
Nebraska	1867
Colorado	1876
North Dakota	1889
South Dakota	1889
Montana	1889
Washington	1889
Idaho	1890
Wyoming	1890
Utah	1896
Oklahoma	1907
New Mexico	1912
Arizona	1912
Alaska	1959
Hawaii	1959

OUR FLAG IS CALLED BY MANY NAMES

The official name for our flag is the Flag of the United States of America.

People often call the flag the Stars and Stripes. Or they may call it Old Glory. That was the name an early sea captain gave the flag of his sailing ship. Today, men in the Navy usually speak of the flag simply as the Colors.

The Star Spangled Banner is the name Francis Scott Key, an American poet, gave our flag more than 145 years ago. The song he wrote about it has become our national anthem or hymn. You have probably sung it many times.

THE STAR SPANGLED BANNER

Oh! say, can you see, by the dawn's early light,
What so proudly we hailed at the twilight's last gleaming,
Whose broad stripes and bright stars, through the perilous fight,
O'er the ramparts we watched, were so gallantly streaming?
And the rockets' red glare, the bombs bursting in air,
Gave proof through the night that our flag was still there.
Oh! say, does the star spangled banner yet wave
O'er the land of the free and the home of the brave?

Francis Scott Key

15

WHERE THE FLAG FLIES EVERY DAY

There are some buildings from which the flag of the United States flies every day.

It flies over a school building, or from a pole in the school yard, during school hours.

If the weather is good, the flag is put up every day on many public buildings. Some of these buildings are — the fire station, the city hall, the police station, and the post office.

The flag flies over the United States Capitol in Washington, D.C. day and night.

It flies over Fort McHenry day and night, except when the weather is bad. Fort McHenry is near Baltimore, Maryland. During the War of 1812, it was bombarded by the British fleet. The Americans defended the fort so bravely that the British could not take it. It was while he watched Fort McHenry being fired upon, that Francis Scott Key wrote our national anthem, THE STAR SPANGLED BANNER.

Because of its importance in our history, Fort McHenry was made a national monument.

SPECIAL DAYS ON WHICH FLAGS WAVE

There are special days on which the United States flag is flown on houses, from public buildings, and often up and down the main streets. Some of these special days are:

LINCOLN'S BIRTHDAY, February 12

WASHINGTON'S BIRTHDAY, February 22

Flags are flown on the birthdays of Abraham Lincoln and George Washington because they were two of the greatest presidents our country has had.

MEMORIAL DAY, May 30

VETERANS' DAY, November 11

Flags are displayed on Memorial Day and Veterans' Day in memory of our fighting men who gave their lives for their country. On Memorial Day, many people go to the cemeteries to put flags on the graves of the soldiers buried there.

FLAG DAY, June 14

People put out flags on June 14 because it was on that day, in 1777, that the Stars and Stripes became our country's first flag.

INDEPENDENCE DAY, July 4

On the Fourth of July flags are seen everywhere. The Fourth of July is the birthday of our country. It was on that day, in 1776, that the Declaration of Independence was signed.

ELECTION DAYS

On election days a flag is put on each building where people go to vote.

OUR FLAG AT SEA

Our country's flag flies from every American battleship. It is put up at eight o'clock in the morning and taken down at sunset. The sailors salute while the Colors are being put up or taken down.

Most ships, other than battleships, fly the flag only while in port. They do not fly the flag at sea.

However, when a ship passes another ship at sea, each raises its flag in salute. This is to show from which country each ship comes.

When a ship at sea is in trouble, it flies its flag upside down. That is one way a ship calls for help.

OUR FLAG IN THE AIR

United States airplanes do not fly the Stars and Stripes. The winds aloft are too strong. Instead, some commercial planes, traveling to other countries, have a flag painted on their tails. Airplanes do not have to carry painted flags, but to do so is useful. It shows that the airplane belongs to the United States of America.

United States Air Force planes do not have an entire flag painted on the tail as do some commercial planes. A star and bars are painted on the plane as shown in the picture.

Parts of the flag are also painted on our navy planes.

HOW TO DISPLAY THE FLAG

Our government has made rules for displaying the flag of our country. These are some of the most important ones.

A flag against the wall on a platform should be above and behind the speaker. The blue field should be at the top and to the left of the people facing it.

If the flag is on a pole on a platform, it must be to the right of the speaker and to the left of the people facing it.

In a parade, the flag is carried in front of or to the right of the marching line.

When a flag is hung over a street, the blue field must be to the north or east.

Sometimes you see a flag on a public building flying half way up a pole. This is called flying at half-mast. A flag flies at half mast when some important American has died.

On Memorial Day, the flag flies at half-mast in the morning in memory of the soldiers who have died. In the afternoon it flies from the top of the pole to honor the soldiers still living.

There are rules for putting up and taking down the flag. It is usually put up early in the morning and taken down at sunset.

When a flag is put up on a pole, it is run quickly to the very top. When it is taken down, it is lowered slowly. It is not allowed to touch the ground.

HOW TO SALUTE THE FLAG

When the flag passes in a parade, we stand very still and salute it. Men and boys hold their hats over their hearts as the flag passes by. Girls and women, and men and boys without hats, put their right hands over their hearts.

Boy scouts, girl scouts, soldiers, and other men in uniform stand with the fingers of their right hands held to the brims of their hats. That, too, is a salute.

Boys and girls salute the flag at school when they pledge allegiance to it. They stand very straight, heels together, heads up. With their right hands over their hearts, they look at the flag as they say:

"I pledge allegiance to the flag of the United States of America and to the republic for which it stands, one nation under God, indivisible, with liberty and justice for all."

WE RESPECT AND LOVE THE FLAG

One of the ways we show respect for our flag is by taking care of it. When we put it up or take it down we do not let it touch the ground. Before we put a large flag away, we fold it carefully. We want to keep it always fresh and bright.

We do not let a flag fly outside at night or when the weather is bad.

If our flag becomes old or torn and faded, we do not throw it out with the rubbish. We think too much of it for that. Instead, we burn it.

Whenever we look at our flag, let us remember it stands for our country. To many Americans, the red and white stripes stand for the unselfishness and the courage of men and women who have served their country well. The blue field, with its stars of white, stands for the freedom for which brave Americans have fought and even died.

Elinor Rees's father was a Welshman educated in France. Her mother was a native Californian. Dr. Rees learned French at home as a child so it is not surprising that she chose the teaching of languages as a career.

Dr. Rees holds a B.A. and an M.A. degree from the University of Southern California. She received her Ph.D. in the fields of English and French from Stanford University. She has also studied at Oxford, at the Alliance Francaise, and at the Sorbonne. She has a teaching diploma from the University of Poitiers, France.

Dr. Rees has taught in various high schools in Southern California. She was an exchange teacher at the Royal Grammar School at Henley-on-Thames for one year. At present she is head of the language department at San Gabriel High School, San Gabriel, California.

Jerome Bowen received his art training at the University of California at Los Angeles. He is currently an artist-designer of animated, industrial, and commercial films.